HOW TO GET THE INTERVIEW CALLBACK AND LAND THE JOB

A GUIDE FOR THOSE STRUGGLING TO GET INTERVIEWS IN THE COVID-19 ECONOMY

PRADIP BHANDARI

CONTENTS

INTRODUCTION

Do you feel like your world has come to an end with the COVID-19 crisis? Are you having trouble finding a new job in the new economy? Are you afraid that you're too old to be back on the job market or unable to find a job at the same level of compensation and rank as your old job? Are you one of the millions who is wondering what exactly you're going to do? How will you provide for your family? It's a frightening time, and it can be difficult to see what you can do to provide for yourself and your family. It's particularly tough if you—like many people—don't have a nice financial cushion saved up to help see you through the crisis.

If you're feeling the fear for any of these or other reasons, you're not alone; over 35 million Americans have lost their job since mid-March, and the UN estimates that the crisis could wipe out some 195 million jobs globally. What's more, the crisis has resulted in a new normal in many workplaces around the world that's likely to affect older workers in mid-level management positions more drastically as the economy cranks back up. These are the workers who are likely to be terminated, and they will also have a harder time finding a new job at the same level of compensation and rank as the one they lost.

Let's face it—it's economically convenient for companies to lay off well-paid workers to save more money in the short term. That then leaves openings for younger workers to move up the corporate ladder, so management won't have to worry about losing fast-track talent. It's a trend known as juniorization, and it can leave you in quite the bind as you struggle to find a new job. Moreover, many companies are flattening their hierarchy by eliminating middle-management positions. It's not just the person who's fired; the entire position ends up being eliminated. Going through with this both saves costs and helps protect upper-management jobs. However, no matter the kind of job you've lost or how old you are, it's a difficult time to be looking for work. You have to have a strategy that meets the challenges of the new economy.

With millions of people looking for work in this post-COVID-19 economy, employers have their pick of people who will accept a lot less money than those more experienced workers. What can you do to make yourself stand out amongst the millions now looking for work and get that callback for an interview?

You can choose to either wallow in self-pity or stand up, learn, act with resilience, and re-enter the job market. It involves taking a few steps back to learn about the situation, so you can understand how to position yourself best to get the job you want. Every crisis comes with opportunities. This book is designed to show you how to identify and take advantage of the opportunities in your business.

The first step in the process is to learn the situation. I'll discuss the new normal for jobs around the world as a result of this crisis. I'll help you understand the skills that can make a difference in finding work in this brave new world. Then, I'll help you put together a new resume and cover letter designed to grab the potential employers' attention. Next, you'll discover how to leverage your experience to find the job that will suit your lifestyle needs best, stand out amongst the many applicants for a given position, and grab a potential employer's attention, so you can get that callback.

And there's more! You'll also discover several tips that can help any job hunter and possible alternatives to the traditional job that you may not have thought about. This book will help you find the hidden opportunities just waiting to be discovered during this crisis.

Why me? I have witnessed the painful repercussions of the current economic crisis personally. I have had to reorient and restructure much of my own business, including re-shuffling talents within my organization in response to this challenging time in history. I have also conducted hundreds of interviews, including during the 2009-2010 recession and swine flu (H1N1) pandemic as well as during the 2013-2016 ebola epidemic. Additionally, as I work for a multinational corporation, I have years of experience screening resumes and picking talents. I know what employers are looking for. That has given me a unique insight into the most useful things you can do to either keep the job you already have or reinvent yourself to find a new job. I have created this book as your guide to finding acceptable alternatives to the situation in which you find yourself. This may not have been the way you envisioned reinventing your life, but it could be the best thing to happen to you. It might even be divine intervention working to jumpstart your life and get you on the path to your true passion.

I'll help you work through the strategies you need to do just that—jumpstart your life and make it even better than before. With a little work and creativity, you might also find yourself living your dream life, something you might never have done were it not for this crisis. With more industries feeling the pinch every day, there's no time to spare to create a new, highly-marketable you for the new economy. Let me show you how to get the callback and land the job today!

CHAPTER ONE: A NEW NORMAL

No matter where you live in the world, COVID-19 is changing your life significantly. This is the first time in over 100 years that we've seen a global crisis having this kind of devastating impact. Aside from the tragic human toll the virus has taken, it is also reshaping the business world. Organizations across the globe have seen their revenues drop precipitously in just a matter of weeks. It's stunning how quickly their revenues have dwindled almost to nothing in some cases. That has prompted many companies to take reactive steps to prevent huge losses. Some have established remote work arrangements, worked to secure their supply chains, reduced employee workload, cut costs, and applied for government support.

With little time to react, businesses are only now looking to identify opportunities that exist in this new economy. There are three primary responses companies are using to match their organizational infrastructure with the emerging and rapidly changing market trends. The goal is to create an agile organization that can adjust its infrastructure, product/service portfolio, or route to market to meet varying demands. Let's look at the following three strategies.

1. Same Product, Different Channel

One response that many businesses quickly adopted was to offer their products or services online rather than in the store. Those that offer physical products can digitize them, and services can be delivered using technology-mediated solutions. For example, the Chinese cosmetics company Lin Qingxuan was forced to close 40% of its stores, including all Wuhan locations. That resulted in sales plummeting by 90%. The company responded by redeploying its beauty advisers quickly as online influencers using digital tools like WeChat to engage customers and drive their sales. They also launched a large-scale, livestream shopping event for Valentine's Day that featured over 100 beauty advisers. As a result, just one adviser's sales in two hours equaled a total of four retail stores. The February sales for the company climbed 120% over the previous year. That's a thriving, agile response.

Nike offers another example. The company was forced to close more than 5,000 directly owned and partner-operated stores around China, bringing its offline business to a sudden halt. Once again, the online operations came to the rescue—Nike used its staff to engage Chinese consumers digitally through at-home workouts. As a result, the company saw a 35% growth in online sales compared to the previous year. This strategy is being used in other countries as well. For example, in the US, Napa Valley vineyards began offering online wine-tasting lessons, resulting in their sales exploding. The Bimber Distillery in London started to deliver whiskey tasting kits to customers and running online events. Of course, educational institutions around the world have also geared up their online courses proactively. While these strategies have been very successful for many companies, there are still other ways that companies have responded.

2. Same Infrastructure, Different Product

While switching to online sales can work for many products and services, there are some demands of which the crisis has simply made disappear. For example, many restaurants, bars, and hotels sit empty. However, while the demand for certain products and services has fallen, others' need is soaring. Therefore, some organizations have taken advantage of this by using their existing infrastructure to produce different products or new services. LVMH, a perfume manufacturer, shifted their production to hand sanitizer instead of perfume, for example. Pernod Ricard, which makes alcoholic beverages, did the same. Car manufacturers such as GM and Ford began using their assembly lines to make ventilators. The Chinese automotive giant BYD Co. switched from making cars to producing millions of surgical face masks each week. Hotel chains like Best Western and Hilton began offering their rooms to hospital staff and COVID-19 patients in the United Kingdom. Like the Panera Bread chain, many restaurants have started offering staple groceries and bread products to their customers.

3. Same Products, Different Infrastructure

Although many companies have seen demand for their products drop, some can't keep up with the market, requiring augmentations to their infrastructure. That can be easier said than done. Thus, several companies are taking innovative steps to help. Amazon, for example, is hiring an additional 100,000 employees in the US to meet the increased demand that has resulted from those homebound, online shoppers. They've partnered with Lyft, whose ride requests have plummeted, to use drivers for delivery, warehouse workers, and grocery shoppers. Walmart is also looking to hire 150,000 temporary employees in the US to meet increased demand. They plan to pay a $550 bonus to their current employees. They're also thinking about hiring people laid off from the hospitality and restaurant sectors to fill their needs. Sweden turned to its laid-off airline workers for fast-track training to help the country's health care system in the fight against the virus. To add, the UK trained thousands of EasyJet and Virgin Atlantic crew and staff in CPR so they could fill temporary jobs in the NHS Nightingale hospitals.

THERE ARE MANY PROACTIVE STRATEGIES THAT companies are taking to save their businesses, which has important implications for workers facing dramatic changes and difficult choices. Like businesses, workers need to be flexible and creative as well. Here are a few strategies to consider that can increase your chances of finding work.

Be Creative

As layoffs expand into almost every sector and business, you have to be willing to be creative in your job hunt. If you've had a successful career until now, it's time to leverage the attributes that helped you do that in unprecedented ways. That could mean several different possibilities, including the following:

- **Be willing to take a job outside of your field or career path for a while.** This can be an excellent opportunity to explore jobs that you may have only considered in the past and those that fit your passions better. In these cases, you may not have pursued them because you got another job. Now could be a great time to rethink those opportunities.

• **Be prepared to telecommute.** This is an excellent option since it doesn't matter where you or the company is located. This strategy can open up your job search to include companies throughout the world. To prepare for this, make sure you have a good internet connection, a good working computer, and a microphone headset, the latter of which can help if you have to make numerous calls or engage in online conferences via platforms like Zoom—the headsets filter out background noise.

• **Leverage your skills virtually.** You might have a hobby or talent that you can turn into a short—or long—term business opportunity. Perhaps you can consult online, create an online course, write an ebook, or provide lessons online. These are just a few of the multitude of possibilities out there for online businesses.

• **Learn about and apply for positions in sectors that are ramping up their hiring.** As already mentioned, several businesses need additional help during this time. There are all levels of positions available. Companies need new managers, employees, web designers, stockers, delivery people, packagers, and much more. These may not be your ideal career path, but they can get you through the crisis and present opportunities for some long-term work that you never considered.

Enhance Your Cover Letter and Resume

We'll discuss these both specifically in the next two chapters. Suffice it to say that your cover letter and resume are critical to getting your foot in the door. Your application documents should emphasize how diverse, cross-functional, and flexible you are as an employee. It's beneficial to list even those talents that might not relate to the job in question directly. For example, you might be applying for a job as a call specialist. Still, if you're accustomed to managing people, writing reports, and using various computer programs as part of your previous post, you should list those skills. You could be perfectly suited for a better position, or the company in question could hire you partially because they see your potential for promotion as management positions become available.

It's also crucial that your application documents list previous experience you might have had with cross-training for various positions. Any training you haven't had not only highlights skills you've developed, but also how you're willing to work as a valuable member of the team, and how you don't mind training to develop new skills, even if those skills aren't directly applicable to the position you're seeking. It's also important to show the company to which you're applying that you've done your homework and researched them. You know how you could fit into the existing organization.

Be Prepared to Interview Virtually

This holds for not only the interview itself but also the application process. It can help to have a video cover letter since many modern companies like to have videos of potential employees. It shows you can handle the technology of putting a video together, introducing yourself succinctly, and speaking eloquently about your skills. That's also true of the virtual interview. For both a video application clip and a virtual interview, there are several tips you can consider that can help make you look professional and persuasive.

- **Dress like you would if you were going to a physical interview.** That means specifically to dress nicely. Such dress may often be overrated, but it shows that you care enough about impressing your potential employer to look professional. You should do this, even if you're just being interviewed over the phone. It will also make you feel more professional.

- **Think about your tone of voice.** You will want to show enthusiasm for the job for which you're interviewing. This is why it's also important to do your homework about the company. The more you know about them, the more they will see you are genuinely enthusiastic about working for them.

- **Make sure the environment in the video with you is clutter-free and well-lit.** You want your potential employer to see that you're an organized, efficient person, and a clean, organized, well-lit environment for your interview will help to communicate that.

- **Make sure you know the job description.** If it's a phone interview, you can have it in front of you as you are speaking to the interviewer. Be sure to point out how your qualifications are a good match for the job requirements.

- **Have questions for the interviewer.** You're not just interviewing to be their employee—you're interviewing *them* as your potential employer. You want to be a good match for the company, so make sure they're right for you too. Also, by having some questions to ask, it shows them you've considered the position carefully and are truly interested.

• **Make sure you download any necessary programs or software updates for video interviews ahead of time and test the equipment.** You do not want to have technical difficulties that cause problems during the interview, particularly if you're being interviewed for a remote or telecommuting position. You will want to show you have full command of the required technology for the position. Also, by practising ahead of time, you can ensure the setup is ideal. You will want to check the volume, camera position, and lighting.

THESE TIPS WILL HELP YOU TO MAKE A GOOD FIRST impression on potential employers. By emphasizing your creativity, professionalism, and flexibility, you have a better chance of standing out as a potential hire. Show off your talent and technological skills and let them see you for the professional you are, and they'll be sure to put you on their shortlist.

CHAPTER SUMMARY

In this chapter, we've discussed the new normal in a COVID-19 world, and we've highlighted how you can stand out from the crowd when applying for positions. Specifically, we've covered the following topics:

• The three general strategies companies are adopting to respond to the changes created by the pandemic;

- The steps you can take to make yourself stand out from the crowd;
- General information to include on your resume and in your cover letter;
- Preparing for virtual interviews;
- Highlighting your skill sets and flexibility; and
- Creating a professional appearance.

IN THE NEXT CHAPTER, WE'LL DISCUSS THE DETAILS OF creating a new cover letter that's sure to get you noticed.

CHAPTER TWO: A NEW COVER LETTER

Many people simply throw together a cover letter without giving it much thought. However, it is critical to getting noticed. The goal of the cover letter is to get the employer to read your resume. On another note, the cover letter is the first impression you will give your potential new employer, so you definitely want it to be good. This is, after all, your shot at selling yourself to the person doing the hiring. You can think of your cover letter as the blurb you find on the back of a book. If that blurb doesn't spark your imagination, you're not nearly as likely to buy the book. Thus, you want a cover letter that shows your potential employer how multi-talented you are, how versatile you are, and how well you would fit into the company's culture. So, to help with understanding how to write a fabulous cover letter, here are a few Dos and Don'ts.

Dos

1. Address the Human Resource Manager or Head of

the Hiring Department by name. If you know their name, use it; if you don't, try searching for it as described in a subsequent chapter on Job Hunt Tips.

2. Insert the company name under the employer's name and title. You want the cover letter to look professional, and the protocol is to include the company name and the employer's name and title.

3. Include the current date. Remember that you want to convey how enthusiastic you are about the job, so you don't want an old date on the cover letter, and you also want the employer to know that you're attentive to details, like including the correct date.

4. Research the company thoroughly. As you write your cover letter, you want to mention how your qualifications address the salient points in the job description. Don't assume the employer will make the connection either; point out how and why you're perfect for the job. Knowing important information about the company also shows your enthusiasm for the job.

5. Mention the company name one or more times in the middle of the letter. For example, you might say something like, "This is why I strongly believe you would find me to be a great asset to the management team of Crowne Export Inc." This re-emphasizes why your skills are a good fit for that particular company.

6. List other variable cross-departmental roles or projects you've worked on to show your flexibility. This is particularly relevant these days since COVID-19 has dramatically changed the job market. Having multiple talents shows the company just how handy you can be, and it assures them of your value to the company. Given the scarcity of jobs at the moment, it's critical that you show how much you have to offer a company.

7. Brag about the additional requirements you meet. If the company wants something else, like local experience, expertise in Java, or a relationship with local authorities, this is where you will want to tell them exactly what you bring to the table in that regard.

8. Emphasize how your skills meet their needs. Don't leave it to the person doing the hiring to put two and two together; tell them exactly how you can help them meet their goals. For example, if they're looking for a Corporate Account Director based in Atlanta, then include in your cover letter the fact that you have, "More than 10 years of sales and account management experience in the Atlanta region." In fact, pick five of the most important skills they are seeking and tell them how your experience makes you highly qualified to fulfill those needs.

9. Give them a bonus: Aside from the five skills you highlighted in the example tip above, list one more bonus skill that you've developed, and that is vital for the company. Using the example above, if you're applying as a sales manager, then write about your marketing job exposure in the first two years of your career. You can even discuss the marketing skills you used on a specific project at your last job. It's important to remember that the company might be cutting positions and could use someone with multiple talents.

10. Use the proper letter format. Aside from formatting the heading correctly as discussed above, end the letter with "Sincerely" and include your full name and contact details. First, doing so shows your knowledge and abilities for writing proper letters; second, it shows that you're courteous; and third, it shows you have an eye for detail.

11. Read the letter from start to finish at least three times. Read it three times to yourself, three times out loud, then have someone read it to you. This will help you catch any typos and/or grammatical errors that could be in the letter. It will also help you judge its feel and flow, which you want to be professional and smooth.

THESE TIPS TELL YOU WHAT TO DO IN YOUR COVER letter, but it's also important to know what *not* to do. Toward that end, let's examine the don'ts of writing a cover letter.

Don'ts

1. Do not use one standard cover letter for all applications. Nothing says you're uninterested in a job quite like using a form letter for each application you're filling out. You want the person responsible for hiring to know you're really interested in their company, so you need to be conscientious enough to tailor your cover letter to their specific job posting.

2. Do not address it to "Dear Sir/Madam" or "To Whom It May Concern." Try to find the name of the person responsible for hiring or the head of the department you would be hired into if you can't find the name of the person on the hiring committee. If you absolutely do not have any luck with finding their names, then write the letter to "Attention, Human Resource Department."

3. Do not try to summarize your resume. This letter is for addressing that which pertains to this specific job. In other words, it's for pointing out how and why you are the best candidate. Your resume lists your skills and previous jobs, but the cover letter tells the person responsible for hiring why those skills are a great fit for the job posting. So, focus on what makes you a good choice for that particular job.

4. Do not make spelling and grammar mistakes. If you make spelling and grammar mistakes, it says two things to your potential employer: first, that you don't have a good command of the language in which you're writing; and second, you don't pay attention to details. Both these messages are terrible to send to someone who is considering you for a job. Even if you're not writing in your native language, you will want to show your potential employer that you will take the time to make sure you get the details right.

5. Do not write about why you want to join their company—write about why *they* should want *you* to join their company. While it's important to show your enthusiasm for working for their company, you will want to focus this letter on why they should hire you rather than anyone else who's applying for the job.

6. Do not write about why you left your past jobs. Whether you left the job or were let go, it's better to focus on why you're the best choice for the job rather than why you left some other job. No matter the reason you left, you just don't want the focus on that topic.

7. Do not write your expected salary unless specifically asked to do so. Don't offer up your expected salary unless they ask for it in the cover letter. If they do ask, give an appropriate range for the position. However, it's better to avoid this situation if possible, since you don't want to box yourself in. It's better to wait and see what their offer is, then make a counter-offer if it's not suitable for your needs.

8. Do not waste space by mentioning how you found the job. They know where they advertised, so there's really no reason to include this information. Often, companies will ask this as part of a survey at some point during the interview process; of course, then you can indicate how you found the position. Otherwise, the cover letter is not the appropriate place for this information.

9. Do not rely solely on the cover letter: The cover letter is just a way to make a good first impression. Its goal is to get the employer to read your resume and request an interview, which is where you can really shine. The cover letter is important, but what will really get you the interview is your resume, and what will get you the job is an impressive interview. The cover letter is merely one step in the process.

By now, you may be wondering what a good cover letter looks like exactly. The example below is presented as one kind of good cover letter. Notice how it fulfills all of the dos and none of the don'ts.

Cover Letter Sample

David Jones
(555) 555-5555 | someone@somedomain.com | PO Box 222 | Sometown, MA 55555

[Current Date]

Hannah Smith
VP Purchasing
ABC Company
15 Main St.
Sometown, MA 55555

Dear Ms. Smith:
As an accomplished purchasing specialist with extensive healthcare industry experience, I was very interested to learn about your purchasing specialist opening. I offer eight years of experience working for XYZ Company, which is a national home healthcare company and a billion-dollar leader in the industry. As the company's corporate purchasing specialist, I managed:

- Purchasing functions for 115 locations.
- 75 major contracts in areas including medications, supplies, equipment, furniture, uniforms, distribution, and vending machines.
- A 15-member team of contractors, buyers, analysts, and support staff.

Consistently recognized for outstanding performance, I saved XYZ Company more than $5.3 million in 2015 alone, and I am confident I can do the same for ABC Company. An expert in contract negotiations, vendor management, and global sourcing, I repeatedly reduced expenditures, cost-of-sales (COS) and cost-of-goods (COG), and assisted with major system implementations of inventory, purchasing, and tracking systems.

I also continue to be active in the American Purchasing Society (APS) and have completed courses in business ethics, contract law, the art of negotiation, and supply chain management. I plan on sitting for the Certified Professional Purchasing Manager (CPPM) exam later this year. Additionally, given my skills as a purchasing specialist, I have always been interested in marketing. Last year, I participated in a seminar on developing marketing skills at the annual APS conference. As a purchasing specialist, I find the art of marketing both interesting and informative for my job, but the seminar also gave me additional skills that may be helpful for improving your company's ability to provide quality home healthcare services in the Sometown region and beyond.

I am confident that my ongoing studies and my diverse skills combined with successful experience in the field will enable me to pursue cost-reduction opportunities aggressively and improve return on investment (ROI) for your company. If you agree that my skills and experience would benefit your operation, please call me at (555) 555-5555 or email djones@somedomain.com to arrange an interview. Thank you for your time, and I look forward to speaking with you.

Sincerely,

David Jones
(555) 555-5555
djones@somedomain.com
Enclosure: Resume

THIS IS A GREAT COVER LETTER SAMPLE BECAUSE IT focuses the reader's attention on all the reasons that ABC company should hire David Jones. It lists his extensive experience, ongoing educational interests, and the diverse skills he possesses that could help the company in multiple ways. In other words, this is a cover letter that will get the attention of the individual(s) responsible for hiring.

CHAPTER SUMMARY

In this chapter, we've discussed how to write a winning cover letter. Specifically, we've covered the following topics:

- The Dos and Don'ts of cover letter writing;
- How to create a cover letter that draws attention to your skills, highlights your attention to detail, and expresses your enthusiasm for working with this particular company; and
- The specific mistakes to avoid when writing a cover letter, including spelling and grammar errors and extraneous information.

IN THE NEXT CHAPTER, YOU WILL DISCOVER HOW TO create a winning resume.

CHAPTER THREE: A RESUME THAT WINS

Once the winning cover letter you've written has convinced the hiring manager to give your resume a quick glance—and I do mean a *very* quick glance—you will want your resume to convey your experience easier and in a way that will capture their attention and convince them to look a little more closely. Most hiring managers will not read every line on your resume, but they will look for particular skills and competencies. They are also trained to scan quickly through resumes, looking for those specific details. Therefore, your resume needs to provide that information in a way that is well-organized, professional, and makes those details stand out.

Once again, in this COVID-19 world we now live in, you will want to put a bit more detail in your resume about multiple skills you possess that could help them in numerous areas of the company. You will want to show them you are talented in many ways that can be a boon for their company. You're not the only one applying, so you have to show them why they should choose *you*. That's why showing them you can go above and beyond the job you're applying for will always be a plus during a crisis like the world is now experiencing. You also want to do this succinctly.

For your resume, you need to remember one important rule—less is more! It's best to make your resume just one page in length; at the same time, it needs to highlight your skills, key information, and your core competencies. While it may sound daunting to reduce all you've done to one short page, it's worth remembering that most CEOs nowadays have a one-page resume. There are a few tips that can help with reducing the length of your resume.

• If you're not applying for a job outside your field, don't list all the responsibilities you had in your previous role. There's no need for that information, and it will just take up space.

• Instead of your responsibilities, focus on your achievements. Don't tell the hiring manager what you did as a Sales Manager for a hotel; instead, tell them what you achieved in that position.

• List additional skills you possess that may not necessarily be relevant to the specific job listed, but that might be helpful in other areas.

Now that we have the general rules in place, let's look at a few specific Dos and Don'ts for creating a winning resume.

Dos

**1. Highlight skills and competencies the employer is

looking for first. List what they want first, then you can add other skills.

2. Write a strong introduction that summarizes your professional signature. You will want something that summarizes you in just a few words. For example, "Go-getter with 10 years experience in Sales and numerous Marketing Awards" would be a great summarizing introduction.

3. Add a little color. Use some colorful and eye-catching visual elements rather than simply boring words to get the attention of the hiring manager. You will want to make your resume stand out, and color helps.

4. Try a free online version of a one-page resume template. There are numerous templates available, so you can find one that suits your style quite easily.

5. List your most recent jobs and education first. You will want to structure your jobs and educational experience from the most recent to the oldest. That way, the employer can see what you've done most recently right away.

6. Instead of listing responsibilities, list achievements. Rather than listing your daily responsibilities under each job title, it's better to list your achievements. Show them what you've accomplished and use those accomplishments to convince them why you're right for their company.

7. Include cross-training and cross-exposure. Just as you did in your cover letter, you will want to show potential employers how flexible you are and just how that might benefit their company. By showing them the areas in which you have some experience, even if they are not your main areas of expertise, you are still letting them know your general flexibility.

8. List only the vital skills and competencies for each role. Don't go into details about other skills at this point; you can always discuss skills in the interview.

9. List the month and year for each job held. When writing out the time period for each job, include the month and year. For example, "From 5/16-2/20."

10. Fill in the gaps. If you have a gap between jobs, it's better to fill that in with what you did rather than leave it blank. You can always write something like "Took time off for family care" or "Education and study," but do not leave that gap blank.

11. Be sure to give your full name and contact information. Don't use nicknames, titles, and/or last names without a first name; include your full name and at least two ways they can contact you—this will usually be your phone number and an email address.

12. Create a neat, clean email address. You will want to have an email address that is not too complicated, and it might help to include some element of your name—for example, JaneDoe35@gmail.com, or J.Do@msn.net. You definitely do not want to have an inappropriate or odd email address—perhaps something you thought was funny when you created it, but it will appear unprofessional to your potential employer. In fact, it may even be a better idea to create a brand new, professional, and simple email address for this purpose.

13. Use the full name of your previous companies. Even if your company was referred to by a shortened name when you worked there, put the entire name on your resume. Again, it is more professional, and there also won't be any mistake about the company you mean.

Now that we've discussed the dos, let's take a look at the don'ts.

Don'ts

1. Do not submit a generic resume with each job application. You want the hiring manager to see that you've taken the time to tailor your resume to their company. That shows genuine interest in the job.

2. Do not make spelling and grammar errors. Just like with your cover letter, if you submit a resume with spelling and grammar errors, it will likely end up in the trash. Making these kinds of errors is unprofessional and displays a lack of education or inattention to detail.

3. Do not use jargon or industry abbreviations. If you know your resume is going to an expert, it may be okay to use jargon and/or industry abbreviations; however, if you either don't know who will be reading your resume, or you know it will be going through human resources first, you will want to avoid this kind of language.

4. Do not list daily responsibilities. It really doesn't help to list day-to-day tasks, especially since it's likely they know what those would have been if you're applying to the same industry. Even if you're not, it's better to list achievements that convey a sense of what you were responsible for doing.

5. Do not list your references. Rather than listing your references—which takes up space on the one-page resume—simply write, "References provided upon request."

6. Unless requested or important for the job, do not include your language skills. Because space is a premium, it's better to leave this out if it won't add to your chances of getting the job. On the other hand, if you're applying to an international company where language skills can be a big asset, then it may be worth including, and there exist several one-page templates with a space to do just that.

7. Do not list all the roles you've held since graduation. Instead, focus on the three most relevant roles for the job you're hoping to get. You can add a fourth one that says something like, "Various sales roles from 2000 - 2003—specific information available upon request."

8. Do not include travel history, hobbies, or other extraneous information. Unless this information is relevant for the job you're applying to, it's not necessary to include it. It takes up space and doesn't really tell the hiring manager much about your skills.

9. Do not put your friends' and family members' phone numbers on your resume. If you include references, they should all be professional references rather than personal ones.

10. Do not use a funky email address. We touched on

this a bit in the Dos section. Your email address, like the rest of your application materials, should be professional. If your email address is something like crazylover3@domain.com, change it or get a new one for the job hunt.

11. Do not put your salary expectation. As with the cover letter, unless you are asked to provide a salary expectation, save it for the interview. If you are asked, put down a reasonable range for your level of experience and the job you're seeking.

THESE TIPS WILL HELP YOU PRODUCE A WINNING resume—one that will get you noticed and push your application to the next stage. Remember that you're not the only one applying, so keep it short, relevant, and professional. If you do that, you'll be sure to get that call back for an interview. Check out the template below for a great one-page resume. Notice that it's eye-catching, well-organized, and provides you with ample space to list all relevant information on one page.

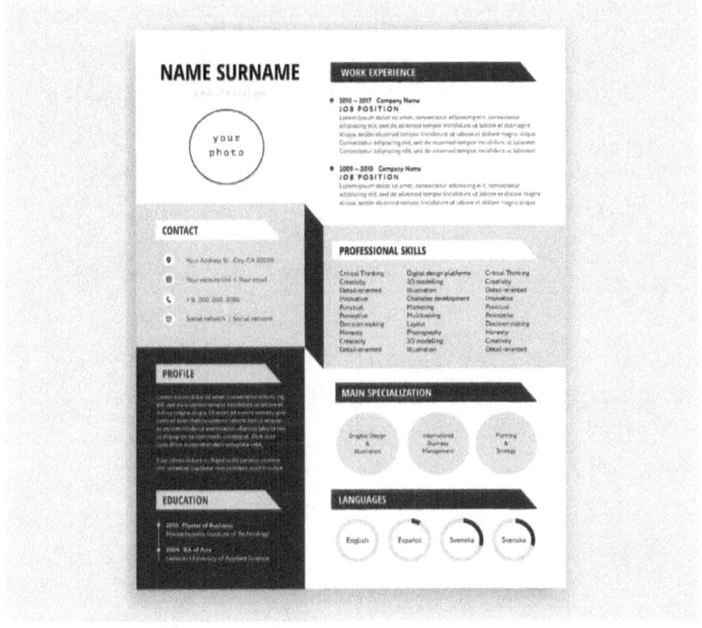

CHAPTER SUMMARY

In this chapter, we've discussed how to create a winning resume. Specifically, we've covered the following topics:

- The importance of a succinct yet powerful resume that conveys all relevant information about your skills and achievements;
- The Dos of resume writing, including listing your achievements instead of your daily

responsibilities, using your full name, and
restricting the length to one page; and
- The Don'ts of resume writing, such as not making
  spelling and grammar errors, not listing
  extraneous information like hobbies or travel
  history, and not using jargon.

IN THE NEXT CHAPTER, YOU WILL LEARN HOW TO MAKE
recruiters see you over other candidates.

It's one thing to write a winning resume and enticing cover letter, but it's quite another to make sure those documents reach the right person. Even if you have the best, most winning content, if your application materials don't catch the attention of the people who set up interviews, you won't get selected. Remember that companies are in a real pinch during this crisis; they need help, and they need it now. They also have tons of applicants to choose from, so if you plan to get selected of an interview, you have to stand out and get your resume into the hands of the person making the decisions. So, let's look at a few things that can help you go from invisible to a superhero!

- **Find out who will receive your resume and who it should go to; then, send it to them too.**

If the advertisement for the job asks that you send the resume to a generic email address or someone who is not in human resource management, then you will want to find out who is the head of human resources and who is the head of the hiring department. I'll have more tips on this for you in the chapter on job hunt tips, but your aim here is to get your resume into the right hands, even if that means drawing outside the lines. Companies often have a screening process whereby the first step is to see if you fit certain minimal requirements. For example, having a bachelor's degree might be a minimum educational requirement. The job of the screener is simply to check a box that says you have met the minimal requirements. If you don't, your resume will be discarded. Your resume has to go through that process too, but that doesn't mean you can't find the name of the hiring manager and send your resume to them too. By taking that extra step, you can impress them with your genuine interest and your ingenuity in finding their name and email address. A lot of job seekers get noticed this way.

- **After sending your resume to the hiring manager or human resource manager, send it to the head of the department for which you will be working**.

When you do this, you should re-write your cover letter as well. This would be a place you can use industry jargon and abbreviations that will tell them you understand the field. You should also mention that you sent your resume through the proper channels, but that you wanted to contact them personally because you're really interested in the job. In the chapter on job hunt tips, I'll lay out several ways you can find the email address for this person, but suffice it to say that even just by taking this extra step, you show enthusiasm for the position. Taking this additional step will also increase your chances for an interview astronomically. I have used this method to my significant advantage over my entire career. It definitely works.

- **If you have taken these extra steps and you're still waiting for a call, make sure you keep going back and refreshing your profile with a few minor changes.**

Doing so will ensure your resume is up-to-date and fresh. It will also call attention to your profile, so recruiters will see you're interested in their position.

- **Avoid cliché words and use specific keywords to help make them notice you.**

Make sure you use industry keywords clearly and noticeably in both your resume and cover letter. You will probably know the keywords in your industry—their use indicates to the listener that the user knows what they're talking about. Use keywords in your resume and list the relevant skills as bolded bullet points under the appropriate heading.

Likewise, you will also want to avoid cliché words and phrases. Some descriptive phrases, like "highly-qualified," are overused and almost no specific meaning. Instead of saying something like "highly-qualified," show the recruiter *why* you're highly qualified by emphasizing your achievements. Remember that recruiters have many resumes to read through, and they spend an average of 6 seconds scanning each one. Therefore, you will want to make sure that the relevant information on your resume stands out.

By using these tips, you will become far more visible to the recruiters reviewing your information for the job. Especially during this time of crisis, you'll need to do everything you can to make yourself seen because there are a lot of people looking. These tips will help you to do just that.

CHAPTER SUMMARY

In this chapter, we've discussed how you can increase the chances that a job recruiter will see your resume. The more you can do to call attention to your application, the more likely you will be to get an interview callback. Specifically, we've covered the following topics that will help you do this:

- Get your resume into the hands of the person who will be making the hiring decisions;
- Send your resume and a new cover letter to the department head who will be your supervisor;
- Avoid cliche phrases that have little meaning; instead, show them your skills by emphasizing your achievements; and
- Keep your profile fresh.

IN THE NEXT CHAPTER, YOU WILL LEARN ABOUT leveraging your connections.

CHAPTER FIVE: LUCKY FOR YOU, IT'S ALSO ABOUT CONNECTIONS

Though it's not always fair, the truth is that sometimes, getting a job is more about your connections than it is your skills. It's helpful to know people who can be influential in helping you get a job. Some of your connections may be able to help you get an interview, whereas others might even be able to help you land the job after the fact (or even without the interview). Either way, knowing the right people can help you greatly while job hunting. In fact, in an environment of corruption, knowing the right person can even get you a job if you don't have the right qualifications. In a corruption-free environment, the right connection can introduce you to the right person, place your resume in the right hands, and influence the recruiter to select you for an interview. Either way, it may sometimes be all about the connections, so you have to learn to leverage your connections usefully.

The following are a few tips that can help you make the best out of the connections you have:

1. Networking: Every professional knows the importance

of networking. You never know when that business card you exchanged as you were sipping a cocktail at the reception will pay off. That's why you want to always have a business card with you and store the business cards you receive in a safe place. You may be able to make good use of that contact as you're looking for a job. It's likely they might not remember you, so don't beat around the bush when in contact. Exchange a few pleasantries—whether over the phone or via email—then hit them with what you need. Don't be afraid to ask for help because they just might know someone who needs someone like you!

2. Ex-bosses: There are many people during this crisis who didn't lose their jobs because of any problem with their work; rather, companies are letting people go to save their bottom line. If you have an ex-boss who can give you a good recommendation, then you can also use that contact to find out more about the department you're applying to now. They may be able to tell you who to contact, help you get in contact with them, and give you a good recommendation. If you have these kinds of connections, use them to your advantage during the current crisis.

3. Friends and family: If you don't have any outside connections that can help you in your search, try asking friends and family. They may know someone either in the department you're applying to or in another company. Also, remember that some of your neighbors may know someone in the department you've applied to or in another company that's looking for new hires.

4. Search online: You can also find connections online. Maybe old high school friends who ended up in the same industry have a connection to a company you've applied to, and perhaps they can help to get noticed by the recruiter. Your network is always bigger than you think.

5. Ask your references: The people you would give as references can be a major networking hub for helping you find work. It's also natural to reach out to them if you're planning on using them as a reference. Contact each of them and tell them what's up. Let them know you would like to use them as a reference and confirm their agreement. Additionally, describe your goals and ask them if they know of anyone who's looking for someone with your qualifications. Then, as you're searching, keep them informed of your progress so you can prepare them for calls from potential employers. Finally, regardless of what happens, thank them for their help with your job search.

ASIDE FROM THESE TIPS, THERE ARE A COUPLE OF important things to remember about networking. It's important to remember that networking is a way of interacting with other people—not a technique for getting a job or a favor. It's about reaching out to share information and asking questions. Here are a few ways that can help you make the process easier and more enjoyable.

- **Be your authentic self**: Authenticity always shows through, and it is an attractive feature. Don't hide your true interests or goals, as that will only hurt you in the long run. Don't feign interest in something because you think others will approve of it; instead, follow your heart, which will ultimately be far more successful and fulfilling.

- **Be considerate**: If you're reconnecting with some of your old friends or colleagues, take the time to catch up before blurting out what you need. They are your friends, so be a good friend back. On the other hand, if you're connecting with a busy professional whom you don't know very well, it's helpful to get to the point so you're respectful of their time.

• **Ask for advice, not a job**: Asking for a job puts a lot of pressure on the person you're talking to, and that's the last thing you want to do. You want your contacts to help you find a job, not feel ambushed. Ask them for information or insight instead of work. If they can help you or know someone who can, they will be much more likely to do so if you don't put them in an uncomfortable position. They don't want to tell you they can't help you, so don't put that kind of pressure on them. Instead, ask if they have any advice that can help, and they should give it to you readily.

• **Get your act together**: Before you start reconnecting with everyone you've ever known, it pays to do a little homework first. Make sure you can articulate coherently what it is you're looking for--is it a reference, a referral, or an insider's take on the industry? Make a list of questions and even write out a statement about what you hope to achieve. Don't read it, but have it ready so you can reference it as you're talking to them. Also, make sure you can update them succinctly on your qualifications and recent professional experience.

THESE TIPS WILL HELP YOU LEVERAGE YOUR connections more effectively and get you noticed by potential employers. Your connections can, in fact, be your greatest allies in the job hunt.

CHAPTER SUMMARY

In this chapter, we've discussed how to leverage your connections, helping you land that job. Specifically, we've discussed the following topics:

- Making use of networking to make connections in your industry;
- Using friends, family, ex-bosses, and potential references as a means of getting advice in your job hunt;
- Searching online to find connections; and
- The proper etiquette when reaching out to your connections.

In the next chapter, we'll discuss the three most important tips for being successful during the job hunt.

CHAPTER SIX: TOP 3 MOST IMPORTANT TIPS FOR A SUCCESSFUL JOB HUNT

It's not always easy to find the right contact, whether you're talking about figuring out who to send your resume to or using a connection to influence your application. After you've put in the work of designing a well-thought-out resume and cover letter, you will then need to get it to the right person. We've already discussed numerous ways to do that, but I want to share some other tips you can use to find the right contacts and connections during your job search.

Tip #1: Business Directories

You probably have a bunch of these for your industry, and now they can really help make a difference. In those business directories, you'll find email addresses and phone numbers at your fingertips to use in your job hunt. Go through and look for the relevant people to help in your application process.

Tip #2: Public Information

There are a number of ways you can use publicly available information to find contact information for the person who will be making the ultimate decision about hiring. First, leverage your social media platforms to look for their email address or other contact information. LinkedIn is a great place to start. Many professionals and companies alike use that platform to list names of human resource managers and heads of departments, as well as give out their contact information. LinkedIn can also help you look for connections that can influence your application. First, find the department head or human resources manager for the position you're applying to; then, look for common connections you have with that person. You can then give a shout out to your common friend, who could help get you noticed. However, you shouldn't stop with LinkedIn.

You can also peruse other social media platforms like Facebook to find contact information for those important decision-makers. You can even do a Google search if you know their full name. That will often pull up contact information as part of their professional profile. It's just as important for the company that potential clients can reach these people, so it's likely you'll be able to find out something online about their contact information.

You can also try the company's webpage. They will frequently have an "About Us" page that lists the names and contact information for department heads and their human resources department. Remember that you will want to submit your application materials as instructed, but there's no harm in sending them to other people who will be making the hiring decisions as well. They also often appreciate your extra effort in getting the job.

Tip #3: Think Outside the Box

If you've tried the tips above and still can't find an email address for the hiring person, it pays to think outside the box. If you know their name but can't find their contact information, you can look for any email address for that company. If you can find even *one* email address, you can see how the company formats their email addresses. For example, maybe they format them as First name.Last name@domain.com, or perhaps it's First name.Last name@company.com. Whatever the case, you can write separate emails and address them to the various possibilities, but don't just write one email and cc the various possible email addresses in the recipient field. That's unprofessional—instead, take the time to send out separate emails to each possible email address. Only one of them will be right.

Another way to think outside the box, if you can't find connections between any of your colleagues or friends and your potential employer, is to look at closely related industries and even competitors. Maybe you have a connection in a related industry, and that connection may know the hiring person for the company to which you've applied. Reach out to people you know in those related industries and ask for help. If they don't know them personally, they might know someone who does. Once again, your ingenuity could really impress the decision-makers.

These three tips can really make a difference when finding connections and contact information for your application. By using a variety of techniques, you're bound to find at least some information that can help you in your search for relevant contacts. The important thing is to not give up until you've exhausted every possibility. It just might make the difference between getting noticed and your application ending up in the trash.

CHAPTER SUMMARY

In this chapter, we've discussed the three most important tips for a successful job hunt. Specifically, we've discussed the following topics:

- Making use of industry business directories to find contacts and connections;
- Leveraging publicly available information for contacts and connections; and
- Thinking outside the box to get your resume into the hands of the decision-makers.

IN THE NEXT CHAPTER, YOU WILL LEARN ABOUT another alternative to traditional job searches.

CHAPTER SEVEN: ANOTHER WAY

While you've been looking frantically for a job during the current COVID-19 crisis, it may not have occurred to you that there is another way. Perhaps you dreamed of it a long time ago, but then you found a job, and those dreams fell by the wayside. This crisis could just be the perfect opportunity to resurrect those old passions. Of course, I'm talking about creating your own business that can replace your traditional job and give you the freedom you've always wanted. Maybe you have a hobby that could become an online business, for example, or perhaps it's always been your passion for opening a restaurant, but you never had the time to implement a plan that could make that dream a reality. This could just be the opportunity you've been waiting to become your own boss. To help with that possibility, I have organized startups into three categories for your consideration. Any one of these might be the doorway you're looking for into a new life.

1. Hit and Run

This kind of business is short-lived, but it's a quick moneymaker, and though it's not sustainable, it also doesn't require long-term planning. Still, the short-term nature of these businesses means there's less chance to recoup your investment if things go wrong. They will still probably help you through the current pandemic if you're successful, but you likely won't have enough to sustain you long-term.

This kind of business, however, can usually be started by watching a few tutorials, then learning the ropes as you go along. An example of something like this might be a business related to the COVID-19 crisis itself. For example, you may set up a business where you make and sell stylish cloth face masks to be worn while out and about. That's something that could make you some quick and good money, but sales may drop once COVID-19 is under control. Still, it could see you through.

2. Susceptible to Sustainability

These types of businesses last longer than the hit and run type. They also have the potential to be sustainable, and also often require less funding. However, they require more planning. Most people who start these businesses get inspiration from their hobbies, and they see a gap in supply and demand for what they want to offer. This kind of business could be built into a life-long pursuit if nothing goes wrong. If you don't do your homework, however, it might not last beyond three to five years.

Doing your homework means investing in proper marketing, making sure there's a market for what you're offering, and doing the day-in and day-out work necessary to make it thrive. That means networking and more networking, leveraging social media as marketing platforms, and making sure what you're offering is of high quality. This kind of business involves your sweat to make it a reality. Most people in these businesses got everything up and running themselves without help from outside investors. An example of this business might be launching an online consulting business in an area where you have particular expertise. It could be something from life coaching to consulting with companies about winning marketing techniques to dramatically increase leads.

3. Sustainability Focused Businesses

The third possible business you could start is one that focuses on the outset of long-term sustainability. This kind requires much more planning and frequently finding outside investors who can put in significant amounts of funding to get the business off the ground. To launch something like this, you'll need to put together a business plan that includes information, such as what you're offering, how it's different from what's out there already, who will buy it, the amount of money it will take to start, the required talent to hire in, and the time frame from start to product launch. This is a much more complicated process, but if you have a good idea and can sell it, these businesses can be long-term sustainable money makers that have a much better chance of survival than the others. For this kind of business, you really need to be a visionary and a risk-taker. Still, if that describes you, this might be your moment.

Of course, every kind of business involves certain risks, and it's worthwhile to do your homework, so you know what those risks are and what it will take to make your business successful. Additionally, all successful businesses have one thing in common: they all have a product or service to sell. That could mean a specialty service niche you identified as lacking in the market, your hobby that you want to turn into a professional career, or an invention you've thought about that can change the world. If you're uncertain about exactly what your passion is in life, now is a good time to sit quietly and contemplate the possibilities. Time is on your side right now, so take some time to brainstorm.

You might write out the various ideas you've had throughout the years and see if something really stirs up excitement in you. Otherwise, you could think about the books you read and the things you like to learn about. Perhaps, some of those are hobbies worth turning into a business. For example, maybe you like comic books, and while you might not have the talent to create a comic book yourself, you could have the talent to create an online shop for comic book lovers. There are a number of ways you might be able to create your own business if you have the right passion for it. However, a time of crisis can be a difficult time to be creative. That's when it's worthwhile to find your peace of mind.

When you're stressed, it makes everything more difficult, including figuring out your passion or coming up with creative ways to start your own business. In fact, researchers in neuroscience have found that creativity plummets when you're stressed. That's because your sympathetic nervous system is busy preparing you to either fight or flee from a perceived danger. When you're fearful because you've lost or might lose your job, your brain doesn't distinguish between that kind of fear and the fear of a lion trying to eat you. Thus, it devotes all its energy to prepare you for survival, which won't help your creativity.

To find some peace of mind, you will need to shift your focus from stress and worry and find a way to accept your situation and stay in the present moment, even if it's uncomfortable. There are several ways to manage stress, many excellent coaches who can help, and various spiritual leaders out there with some great advice. However, a few, in particular, stand out. I invite you to invest a little money into some of the better writers on the subject of peace of mind. The following books are well worth a small investment for a long-term benefit that will serve you well in any crisis:

1. *The Power of Now* by Eckhart Tolle
2. *Neuroscience of Change* by Kelly McGonigal
3. *Buddha's Brain* by Rick Hanson
4. *Full Catastrophe Living* by Jon Kabat-Zinn

The best thing you can do to survive this pandemic and any future crises is to find the peace of mind that will help you truly enjoy your life's journey, no matter where that journey takes you. That is the way to survive and thrive.

CHAPTER SUMMARY

In this chapter, we've discussed alternatives to applying for a new job. Specifically, we've discussed the following topics:

- The three different types of startup businesses;
- What is involved with each type;
- Finding a passionate product or service to sell; and
- Finding peace of mind for long-term life satisfaction.

FINAL WORDS

Crises come and crises go, but there are always hidden opportunities in challenging times. This book has been designed to help you identify your options and make the best choices to realize your goals. When you're one of perhaps several hundred applicants, you have to find a way to stand out. There are many different ways you can do that, but as we've noted throughout this book, there are some basic strategies you can take to improve your chances.

By creating a professional, winning resume with an attention-getting cover letter, you can be sure to catch the eye of hiring managers and department heads. You should always highlight your achievements and don't be afraid to brag about your skills. Job markets are always tight, but never more so than during a crisis such as COVID-19. With so many people out of work, you have to make use of every trick in the book to find your way through the storm. That might even mean starting your business and becoming your own boss.

This book has been designed to help you do just that. By using the tips presented in this book, you'll stand a much better chance of catching the eye of the people making the decisions about hires. You've learned how to create professional application materials, leverage your connections, find contacts who can help you get noticed, and even discover a passion that could become a long-term sustainable business.

This crisis might have been an unwelcome disruption in your life, but there are always hidden opportunities just waiting for someone like you to notice and run with. You've learned how to do that in this book, and now it's time to get up and get moving on to your new and improved life. Start by finding the peace of mind that will see you through any storm and end by creating a new reality where you have the job of your dreams. As the famous political slogan says, "Become the change you want to see." Don't let COVID-19 keep you from realizing your dreams. You now have the knowledge you need to land your dream job or find your passion for turning into your own business. Why not get started today?